Hello. Mom? It's Gigi

A Daughter's Quest for Truth

Regina "Gigi" Hodges

Hello. Mom? It's Gigi
A Daughter's Quest for Truth
Regina "Gigi" Hodges

This is an autobiographical work and stories, observations, anecdotes, and memories are to the best of the author's recollection or as shared with her.

Published by Pecan Tree Publishing
Hollywood, FL 33020
www.pecantreebooks.com
info@pecantreebooks.com

ISBN: 979-8-9864215-5-1 Paperback
ISBN: 979-8-9864215-6-8 Ebook
Library of Congress Control Number: 2022919079

Edited by: E. Claudette Freeman
Interior and Cover Design by: Marigold2k
Photo gallery photos are property of the author and should not be used without permission

Pecan Tree Publishing
www.pecantreebooks.com

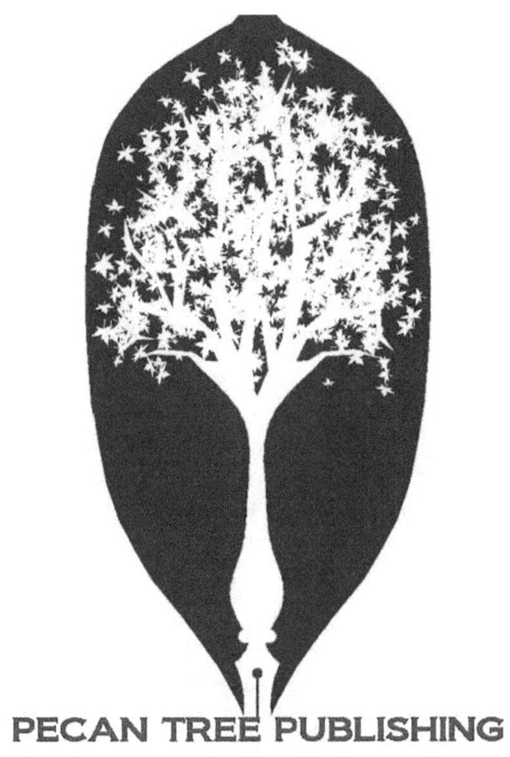

New Voices | New Styles | New Vision
Creating a New Legacy of Dynamic Authors and Titles
Hollywood, FL

This work is dedicated to ...

My mother, Elizabeth Clay Hopkins-Redding who carried me for nine months and gave me a chance at life. Because of her, I am. Mom, as long as I live, you will never be forgotten!

My sister Deborah L. Hopkins-Simmons who departed this life November 8, 2013. Sis, I miss you every day. I take solace in knowing you are no longer in physical or emotional pain. I love you!

In loving memory of my brother Donnell Solomon who transitioned from this life, October 22, 2021. I miss our phone calls, brother.

To my wonderful husband Lamar, who has stood the test of time! You have been by my side through thick and thin, in sickness and health, in good times and bad, for richer and for poorer. Whether we ate a steak or Ramen noodles! I have been able to get to where I am today because of your undying and unwavering love and absolute devotion. Thank you for being my sounding board. Thank you for allowing me to bounce my ideas off you. Thank you for listening to me explain a character I was developing or a backstory. Thank you for letting me read aloud the chapters in this book in their infancy. You, sir, are an amazing man; and I could not ask for a better person to accompany me the rest of the way. I love you with everything in me. Thank you!

To my children, Kevin, Felicia, and JR, I hope you all know how much I love you. When I was at my lowest, you three gave me a reason to continue to live. I pray abundant blessings over your lives and the lives of your children. Many days I prayed that God would allow me to live to see you all grown. He has not only granted that but allowed me to see your children and a great-grand! Won't He do it?

To my nieces Lula and Stephanie, thank you for adopting me as your mother and not just your aunt. Since your mother Debbie has been gone, you ladies have made sure to shower me with love and undying affection. Losing her was traumatic for us all. Your willingness to drive hours to see me several times a year has been far more than I ever could have hoped for!

To my great-nieces, Brittany, Neeshuh, and Bri, thank you all for checking on me and staying connected. It means the world. To all my nieces, nephews, grands, great-grands, I love you all so much.

To all my siblings and cousins, I love you all to life. Let's fight to get connected and stay connected for all the generations that are coming after us!

Special Thanks

I am grateful and thankful to God for the people He has placed in my life to assist me on this journey called life.

To my beautiful and sweet cousin, Barbara. If it had not been for your persistence in staying in touch trying to bridge this awful gulf in our family, this book would not have been written. It was the farthest thing from my mind. It was only after one of our many phone calls and a conversation about my mother that this book was birthed! I thank you for introducing me to my mother. Because of you, I discovered so many things about her that I never knew. I thank you for your kindness and your love. You are heaven sent and I love you with all my heart!

To my wonderful lifelong friend, Rosie Moore. What can I say? God did a thing when he placed you in my path! For over 40 years we have been more than friends. You are my sister. Thank you for always being there, praying for me, teaching me, guiding me, and loving me and my family.

To Carrie Elizabeth Green! You are another lifelong friend. We have maintained our friendship for over 50 years! Whew, that's a long time! I will never forget how you rescued me and my children from being homeless. You took us in and made us comfortable even at the risk of losing your place! Your family has always been my family. I wanted to steal your mother and keep her all for myself! There was no one like Missionary Elvira Green. May she continue to enjoy heaven!

To Pastor Leroy Smith and Lady Smith, thank you for the years of teaching and imparting truth and wisdom into my life. Sometimes the children act like they don't hear when the parents are speaking. But sir, I hear your voice even now instructing me how to go through! Pastor Smith, I am forever grateful to you for encouraging me to seek professional help when I thought I could not go on. Thank you. I love you.

To Pastors Charles and Marilyn Turner, thank you both for always speaking into my life. I thank you for your loving support and your covering of prayer in all that I endeavor to do. Thank you for always showing up at every show I was in or produced! Your friendship and your love have been a constant and for that, I am grateful.

Acknowledgements

To all the many friends who have stayed in the fight with me. Thank you!

To all my surrogate sons and daughters, thank you for your love!

To Andre Sartin and Lionel Nelson, thank you for the many days that you talked me off the ledge. You are indeed my brothers and I love you both!

To Reverend Yvonne Strachan, I will never forget the days I felt alone and cast aside, and you would call at the right moment. Thank you for talking and praying me through those difficult moments!

To Tuwana M. Dumond and Rose Cadeau, you encouraged me to get this book done, thank you! Y'all stayed on me hard and stuck close. I thank you both so much! Those calls of encouragement helped me tremendously.

Finally, but certainly not least, thank you E. Claudette Freeman for taking this journey with me. There were days I wanted to quit. When it became too painful, you pushed me anyway. Thank you for the push. The baby is here!

Applause For Hello. Mom? It's Gigi. And Regina "Gigi" Hodges

"When I think of Regina, I think of royalty. Regina means queen. Regina rules like a queen. Regina protects like a queen. Regina has suffered like a queen; yet she has also triumphed as a queen. I think it's her resiliency and passion combined that makes her such an extraordinary woman of excellence. As you read this book, it will be clear that Regina has a light that shines within her, and that light is called love. I am honored to know and be a recipient of her love."
Dominique Price Dumervil- Educational Specialist and Author

"This story is a much-needed recourse for the motherless child, whether teenager or adult, who is struggling to overcome their pain caused by a turbulent past. Gigi, who I know to be a woman of grace, honor, and generosity, courageously shares her painful story of abandonment in a way that incites the reader to forsake bitterness and embrace forgiveness and healing. *Hello. Mom? It's Gigi* is so relevant for such times that we are in."
Pastor Marilyn Turner, New Hope Worship Center, Miramar, FL; Author, Playwright, Actress, CEO of Marilyn Turner Productions

"Writer Regina Hodges has crafted a gripping tale encompassing family separation, hurt, pain and eventually awakening to a restored place of forgiveness that shines as a rainbow when a daughter finally comes to terms with the impact her mother caused on their relationship. "Hello. Mom? It's Gigi - A Daughter's Quest for Truth" is a spirited eye-opener for those faced with the emotion of disavowed parental love, the tragedy of family disappointment, but the journey to redemption discovered when the inevitable

has been found and creates a lasting joy in a daughter's strained relationship with her mother."
Teddy Harrell, Jr. Assistant Center Director, African Heritage Cultural Arts Center Miami, Florida

"Lady Hodges (as she is affectionally called by me), is a wonderful person whom I call my friend. Knowing her backstory is a perfect example that you don't have to be a victim of your circumstances. I have known Regina for several years; she is a person who is loving, energetic, loyal, confident, and true to her word. I have so much respect for her because despite what she endured growing up, she was able to transform the pain of not knowing her mother, into becoming a phenomenal woman of great character!"
Lionel Nelson – Playwright, LJN Productions

This story of Regina "Gigi" Hodges is one of perseverance and defying the odds. Often you look at a person and hear of their journey and wonder, "how could this have happened to someone," but Gigi has overcome difficulties and fought to stay strong and true to what she believes. Hello. Mom? It's Gigi, is her quest to find the truth about the mother who abandoned her, and in doing so, she has found the strength to forgive. I'm proud to know her as my friend.
Andre Sartin, Producer, Act 2 Stage Productions

Contents

Introduction

This book was written as a labor of love to honor the memory of the woman who gave me life. It has been a tedious journey! It is my hope that it will encourage every person who reads it, to have a better understanding of how unresolved issues hold us hostage. Anger, pain, hurt, disappointments, disillusions, unforgiveness and indifference surrounding those things we choose to avoid makes a significant difference in every aspect of life. Whether we address it or choose not to, as I did for many years, it still powerfully affects us.

I lived in indifference. It was a shield that kept me from addressing issues with my estranged mother Elizabeth, while I had the time to do so. Unforgiveness would not allow me to visit my mother between the ages of 18 and 27. That was a decade of time to ask the questions that plagued me as a child. Even if I didn't get the answers I wanted, at least she would have had a chance to tell her story. But it didn't matter to me.

I didn't allow myself to think about her. If she crossed my mind, I pushed thoughts of her down. I used my indifference as a safety mechanism to guard my heart. A decision I now regret.

I lived this way for years not allowing myself to feel things too long before moving on. Indifference at its finest.

It became easy, after a while, to walk away from people for what I deemed a slight infraction! Not that I didn't like people, but I lived waiting for the other shoe to drop. I lived trusting that whoever came into my life was going to leave eventually anyway.

I struggled with low self-esteem. I was timid and afraid. I had no confidence in my ability to do things, so I was reluctant to try. I didn't believe I was lovable. My own mother didn't love me. The residue of my earlier years was alive and well and I wore it like a badge of honor. Finally, I had to go before God and honestly walk in my truth, giving all my cares to Him so that my healing could begin.

My first order of business was to forgive my mother for being an uncaring woman who walked away from her children. Girls no less. That is what I defined her as — an uncaring woman. My forgiveness journey came after she had been deceased for 33 years.

If there is anyone in your life who you are estranged from, and they are still alive, find the strength to have a conversation while you can. Ask God to help you to forgive and if it is possible, go to that person (or those people) before it's too late. You may not get the answers you want, but healing, for you, can only take place by acknowledging what is wrong, and finding the faith and strength to forgive. Living with regrets is not an easy thing to do. It will eat at you even if you don't think it is. Unforgiveness is like a cancer. It slowly eats at your heart until you feel nothing.

Forgiveness is necessary. Restoration is possible. But reconciliation is healing. Today, I am at peace with myself and at peace with the memories of my mother. It is my endeavor to not allow her birth, life and presence on this earth be for naught.

So, I say her name, Elizabeth Clay Hopkins-Redding.

Regina "Gigi" Hodges

Prologue

Circa 1960

An incredibly attractive petite, African American woman named Elizabeth has boarded a double-decker Greyhound Bus. She laughs incessantly with a group of Navy sailors. They are joking and drinking from varying bottles of alcohol. The sailors are dressed in their military uniforms heading back to base. The noise level has finally reached the driver and he has had enough. The group was having such a good time, they didn't notice that the bus was coming to a full stop on the side of the road.

The bus driver pulled the bus over, parked, stood up and walked toward the back of the bus. The Navy sailors aboard began to quiet down as the driver made his way down the aisle. The woman, traveling with two young girls was laughing loudly with one of the sailors not noticing the approaching driver. It was obvious to the driver that they were all drinking which was absolutely prohibited aboard the bus.

The driver stood in the aisle looking at them with disdain before he finally speaks to the young woman. "If you don't quiet down, I will be forced to remove you from the bus."

The other passengers listened intently as the woman quieted down realizing that she could not be thrown off the bus in the middle of the night with her two girls despite the fun she was having with the sailors. She complied with the driver, he returned to the driver seat, cranked up and pulled the bus back on the highway and drove off into the night.

The bus became eerily quiet the duration of the trip. Over the loudspeaker the driver announced, "Hartford, Connecticut ladies and gentlemen. This is your final stop. Please have your baggage claim ticket available to retrieve your luggage; and thank you for traveling with Greyhound"

Everyone began to exit the bus single file. Elizabeth looked at one of the sailors and smiled, "see you 'round." She reached for her girls, commanding, without the smile in her voice she gave the sailor, "let's go."

"Don't waste your time in anger, regrets, worries, and grudges. Life is too short to be unhappy."

– Roy T. Bennett

CHAPTER ONE

Regrets

"It's been 12 years since the day you got on that bus and casually walked out of our lives. Twelve years! What happened? How could you leave two little girls, your babies, with a neighbor? You didn't think enough of us to at least leave us with a family member? Your own sister? Daddy left us with you! You just casually left us behind without any regard to our well-being. Why? What was so important that you went away for an entire weekend and then chose to stay so long, that your sister (who randomly came to see us) discovered that you were gone-without us! How could you do that? We were your responsibility! What decent parent, mom, or dad, does that?

Why did you let him take us from you? Did you even fight to get us back? Were we not worth fighting for? Did you not have enough love in your heart for your own children? Do you have any idea how your decision affected my life? Debbie's life? Do you know the pain and anguish it caused us? You missed my birthdays. You missed me turning into a young woman. What were you doing all that time? Did you even care?"

That's what I imagine I would have said to her if I had taken the time to go to my mother after I turned 18. Still, I can't help but wonder if the conversation would have gone another way. Would she have been opened to answering all my questions or would she shut me down? I didn't bother because I was afraid of the latter.

Would she have been remorseful or attempt to justify her behavior? Had I gone at that time, and she showed no remorse, sorrow, or shame, it would not have gone well - I can assure you! I can only hope that I would have gotten tears, apologies, hugs, or some type of positive, forgiving emotion. Had she done anything other than that, we might've fought! I think somewhere deep down inside I wanted to hurt her as much as she hurt me. A good slap across the face would have made me feel better.

It's one thing to lose a parent to death but having her alive, living, breathing for years as if we didn't even exist, was worse than death. Growing up with the feeling of disconnect, not belonging anywhere, looking for love and acceptance anywhere and everywhere, was a struggle affecting everything I thought and did! I have wondered over the years had my first family been intact, a loving mother and father, how different my life might have been. What could I have become? What have I become?

The overwhelming feeling of not being wanted, especially by my mother, was a horrible experience. I would not wish it upon anyone. How could I expect anyone to love me if the person who gave me life and was supposed to, didn't? To overhear her say she was leaving and not taking us with her was painful. I don't know all the circumstances. I was too young to understand. Maybe she thought it was a good idea at the time. Maybe she regretted it later.

It made me question and distrust everybody. I felt alone, isolated, trapped in my own mind, even invisible at times. There was nowhere to go with those feelings. No one I could turn to, so I learned to exist inside my own world, not speaking to anyone about how I was feeling. It was an invisible fight. I was air boxing but hitting nothing. I convinced myself that if she didn't want me, then I didn't need her. Indifference became my go to.

I will never know the answers to all my questions. The conversation, the release I have wanted to have has been a one-sided conversation. I waited too late. As I pen this book, I am learning of my mother's journey, and it has become painfully clear to me that her life was full of trauma that only allowed her to exist inside her own world where it was emotionally safe. My journey has been eerily like hers.

According to Substance Abuse and Mental Health Services Administration SAMHSA's National Child Traumatic Stress Initiative, "children of trauma often feel guilt or shame, become anxious or fearful, experience depression and or isolation. We buy into the notion that we did something wrong. Do we beg the question, what's wrong with me? And we live in a perpetual state of why."

I am on a spiritual journey that will allow me, not having ever spoken to my mother, to put these questions to rest. What I know is, I did nothing wrong. It's not my fault. I am worthy of love. I am lovable. I have a voice. Do I regret not seeking her out? I do. Although I don't live inside that regret, it is the biggest one I have. I wish I could go back in time and meet her. She meant well. But her own trauma dictated her path and embedded its pain in me.

"The tragedy of life is what dies inside a man while he lives."

- *Albert Schweitzer*

CHAPTER TWO

The Tragedy of Liz

Elizabeth Clay was born in Richland County, South Carolina December 24, 1934. She had one sibling (that I know of), an older sister, Ethel Clay Williams. Mama was only two and Ethel was three when they lost their mother. They were raised by their grandmother, Cressie Kearse.

Elizabeth was a petite woman, short in stature, with a beautiful smile and large bright eyes and a boisterous voice. I'm told that she was a fierce dresser and being a cosmetologist, always kept her hair done. I have a picture of the short haircut she was known to sport! She looked so polished. She was a singer, and her nickname was "Sangie." She loved reading romance novels.

She and my father separated when I was quite young, eventually divorcing. They were forced to marry, and my father resented that. She was 16 years old and pregnant. Auzzie was 26 and in the Army. He was a strikingly handsome young man and she fancied him. Somehow, they managed to meet up with each other unknowingly to her father. When she discovered she was pregnant, she was afraid to tell her father, but she had too.

As a creative being, I further imagined and built a story of her life during this rollercoaster ride of pregnancies and marital turmoil. This is also based on what I've learned of her and experienced as a woman that reads like...

"Daddy, I'm pregnant."

Her father would not hear of his teenage daughter disgracing the family name by being pregnant out of wedlock. Her father stormed up to the Army base to speak with the Commanding Officer.

"Your soldier has gotten my teenage daughter pregnant and there better be a marriage license in the next three days or there will be trouble."

Shortly thereafter, the two were forced to marry. The marriage started on horrible grounds because of the pregnancy and the forced relationship. Soon after they exchanged vows, the physical abuse began.

She lost the baby that forced marriage. That child was a boy. Three months later, she found herself pregnant with her second child. This time a girl - Debbie. Within four months of this birth, she was pregnant again. Another boy. He lived exactly 10 hours and 35 mins. Two years after his death, she was pregnant with her fourth child -another girl - Regina

Liz sat in her car sobbing after getting the news that she was once again with child.

"I just can't bring another baby into this world, my world. Oh God! What am I going to do with another baby?"

Perhaps she cried not at the fact that she was pregnant, but the timing couldn't be worse. She had been pregnant for three years in a row and if the two boys had lived, by the time this new baby would arrive, she would have four children by the age of 22.

The trauma of having no voice in the decision to wed, losing both her sons, and enduring harsh physical abuse was too much for Liz. The last thing she needed was a new baby as she planned to leave Auzzie. She was mentally and physically tired. Being on her own with one child was scary enough but two? She sat in that car and pondered what she should do.

"What am I going to do?"

The tears rolled down her face. At last, she resolved to stay put - at least until after the baby was born. Her little girl would be four years old by the time the new baby came. She would work on a plan of escape.

Sadly, it would be another four years before she and Auzzie separated. By this time, she was drinking heavily. Auzzie left Liz and the girls and moved out of state.

Their beginning and history considered, his leaving could have been an answer to Liz's prayers; however, by the time he left, she was lost emotionally and mentally.

Liz decided to take a quick getaway, leaving the girls in the care of a neighbor. By the time she returned, she discovered she had lost her surviving children. She was devastated. The only thing tangible from the tragedy of her teenaged thrust into marriage and family was the daughters who were now gone. She took solace in the bottle.

That's what I imagine as I think about that trauma which shrouded her; that she unfortunately and tragically shrouded her seed in. Mom eventually moved from South Carolina to Hartford, Connecticut, and resided there until her passing October 8, 1985, at the youthful age of 50.

"An aunt is a safe haven for a child. Someone who will keep your secrets and is always on your side."

– Sara Sheridan

CHAPTER THREE

Auntie's House

I was born and lived briefly in Columbia, South Carolina in 1956. Columbia is the capital of South Carolina and is the second largest city in the state. Columbia is often abbreviated as Cola leading to its nickname as Soda City. Columbia is the site of Fort Jackson, the largest United States Army installation for Basic Combat Training. My father was previously stationed there.

My mother and father (Auzzie) separated when I was about two or three, and my sister Debbie around six or seven. My mother had a drinking problem. That problem, supposedly, contributed to his leaving. Between the physical abuse, mom's smoking, and drinking, coupled with the resentment issues, the marriage was in constant turmoil. During one of the seasons of high turmoil, while my parents were apart, mom was living her life and having fun with Debbie and I in tow. That changed one day out of nowhere. Mom took a break from her responsibilities and daughters, much to everyone's surprise.

My aunt Ethel (mom's sister) had not heard from my mother in a few days, so she decided to go to the house to check on us. As she approached our home, the owner of the daycare (I don't know her name so I will call her Miss Sally) called out, "Hey! She's not there."

My aunt responded, "what do you mean, she's not there? Where is she?"

Miss Sally worried, replied, "I don't know. She's been gone for a while!"

Auntie inquired, "Awhile? Where did she go and where are the girls?"

Miss Sally calmly said, "I don't know where she went, and the girls are with me."

Auntie was flabbergasted as she made her way across the street, entered Miss Sally's house, and retrieved Debbie and me. She placed us in the car and got into the driver's seat. I was too young to remember if Auntie said anything on the ride back to her house. Once we arrived at her house, she took us inside and got us settled in. I don't know how long we were there, but I have memories of playing with my cousins. My aunt had four children of her own, two girls and two boys. Mitchell, who was the oldest and the same age as Debbie, Francis, who was about five months older than me, Clyde, and Brenda, who was the baby. Auntie instantly went from four children to six!

We lived in an area called Greenview. There was a wooded area in the neighborhood, and we would pick bullets (a grape like fruit), and blackberries. One day, while we were out doing just that, Auntie called my daddy to ask for financial help since there were so many of us. Instead of sending money, he found his way to Greenview and took us, returning her head count to four.

That began the separation from our family in South Carolina. We became wandering strangers to my aunts and all my cousins on both sides of the family.

We were off to live in Delray Beach, Florida.

"*Florida, where summer lasts six months twice a year.*"

– Unknown

CHAPTER FOUR

Off to Florida

I certainly understand why it's called The Sunshine State. With its greenery and beautiful palm trees and with no changing of seasons, it is always warm. The beaches are miles and miles of white sand and beautiful water. Daddy never took us to the beach so it would be years before we experienced just how beautifully relaxing those waters could be.

My father was living with his brother, Walter, and his wife Claudia in Delray Beach. I loved my uncle! He was a barber and walked with a limp. As a boy he had stepped on a rusty nail and began walking on his toes refusing to put his heel down. His foot grew abnormally because of that, causing the limp. He also sang and played the guitar. I loved to hear him sing. Debbie told me that he was in a singing group at the church we attended. The others in the group were our dad and the pastor of the church.

My aunt was not a nice lady. She was void of affection and mean spirited. I remember one day she prepared breakfast: bacon, grits, toast, and eggs over easy. I had never had eggs like that before and I refused to eat them!

I was about to scrape the food from my plate into the trash when she angrily said, "I know you're not throwing that egg in the garbage!"

I said, "I don't like eggs like that."

She said, "you will sit down and not leave that table until you eat them, or I will beat your behind!"

I took the beating! I quickly learned from that egg experience not to cross her, so I did what I was told. I learned to eat her runny, yucky eggs, and I stayed out of her way as much as possible.

The best part about being there was my uncle. He would sit on the front porch and play his guitar and sing! I'm sure I sang along. Daddy once told me (during a rare father- daughter moment) that I was singing before I could talk! Uncle Walter was a gentle man with an easy on the ears voice. I loved the way he would call my name. "Gina (as he would call me), you alright?"

I would respond, "yes sir." What I really wanted to say was, "I'm okay now that you're home."

My aunt kept a nice house though; with lovely things in it. She was a housekeeper for rich white people and perhaps the things she had in the house, vases, figurines, whatnots, were given to her. You could admire them, but you had better not touch anything! That called for a beating.

Most of the time spent with my uncle and aunt is hazy but I do remember starting school at S.D. Spady Elementary. The school was not too far from where we lived on the corner of Roosevelt Street and Northwest Third Street. It was a simple looking neighborhood. The houses had flat roofs and most had circular driveways. Nothing fancy. My uncle's house is still there to this day.

There were no buses to take us to school at that time, so we had to walk. You had to be careful walking through those bushes, otherwise you would get sandy spurs on your shoes and socks! Sandy spurs are little sticky ball-shaped thorns that grow in weeds and bushes. You must be careful attempting to remove them to keep them from sticking in your flesh. If one broke in your skin, you would have to get a safety pin, burn it with a match to sterilize it and remove the spur. It hurt like the devil and if the stem broke and stayed in your skin, it would fester and get infected! I had some days like that! I hated those things. They were so bothersome.

Even with this new adventure, I was missing my mother so much and every day, I waited, hoping she would come back to get us. She wasn't mentioned in the house. I never heard daddy talk about her; and Debbie and I didn't talk about her either.

> *"Being a preacher's kid is not for the faint of heart. The pretense of being perfect carries a lot of weight."*
>
> *– Gigi Hodges*

CHAPTER FIVE

The Preacher's Kids

At some point we moved from my uncle's home to the home of my father's new love. Her name was Alice. (Of course, we called her Miss Alice.) When I was growing up, children were taught, especially in the South, to call adults Mister, Misses, or Miss. We were not allowed to call adults by their name. It was disrespectful! Miss Alice was short, with caramel colored skin and a mole under her nose. She was thick with bowed legs.

She was a genuinely nice lady. She had two daughters of her own who would become our new sisters, Frankie and Yvonne. They both were much older than Debbie and me. Frankie was 17 and had a son, Tony. Tony was three years old and had kidney issues. I distinctly remember tripping over the tubing for his port for dialysis and accidently pulling it out. I was so hurt that I hurt him. Tony passed away when he was 17 years old.

We lived in a two-story building in an apartment on the first floor, with dad and Miss Alice. I don't remember much about Yvonne. In 1992, Frankie would reappear in my world when I moved to Delray as an adult. Debbie had found her way back to them when she became of age. I got to see Miss Alice before she passed in 1994. Debbie took me to her house. She was so happy to see me, and I was glad to see her! She hugged me and we sat down and talked a while. It was quite a reunion.

While we were kids in the same home, we attended Ridley Temple Church of God in Christ. I loved that church. The pastor, Elder Ridley, and his wife, lived in a house right next door. I remember the shut-ins back then. That's when you go to church on Friday night and not come out until late Saturday night! The grown-ups would start with singing like a regular Sunday morning service. Someone would read a scripture and expound on The Word. Then another would sing, and after a while, they would kneel for prayer. They would pray around the clock for a whole day and night. The children could bring books or a quiet game. The adults would bring quilts and pillows for the children to make pallets (makeshift beds) either on the floor or on the benches where we would sleep while they prayed. Those were the good ole days. Church was a big part of our lives, and we spent most of our time there. My father became an ordained minister during that time. He sure could turn a phrase when he preached! He could sing your socks off too.

It appeared that this was going to be our new life. We were settling in, going to church and school. It wasn't bad at all. It finally felt like a normal family life. The next thing I recall, is being on that double-decker Greyhound bus with my mother and a bunch of sailors.

Over the loudspeaker the driver announces, *"Hartford, Connecticut ladies and gentlemen. This is your final stop. Please have your baggage claim ticket available to retrieve your luggage; and thank you for traveling with Greyhound"*

Everyone began to exit the bus single file. Elizabeth looked at one of the sailors and smiled, "see you round." She reaches for her girls, commanding, without the smile in her voice she gave the sailor, "Let's go."

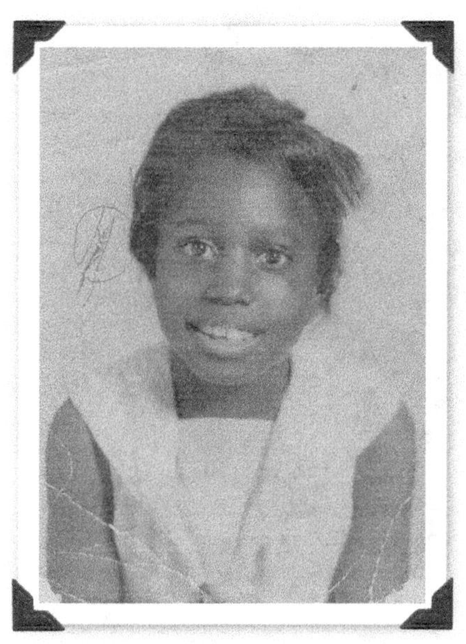

U.S. COAST GUARD

PASTOR ANDREW W. RIDLEY

I like coffee,
I like tea,
I'd like for Janey
To come in with me.
1, 2, 3, 4, 5...

CHAPTER SIX

Double Dutch

We were in a brand-new place called Hartford, Connecticut. *Up north* as the southerner's would say. My mother had kidnapped us from my father! Her getaway vehicle was that double-decker Greyhound bus that we almost got kicked off of! What I remember was living in a high-rise building. It seemed that we may have lived on the 5th or 6th floor. I don't know if I had ever seen a building that tall before. It was also strange to me, how they hung clothes on the clothesline. The line was on a pulley that you had to lean out of the window, pull the line to you and hang the laundry! That was scary.

The neighborhood where we lived was nestled in a community with sidewalks on both sides of the street. That is where I get my love of neighborhoods with sidewalks! Ironically, the home I purchased is in a community *without* them!

The way our lives were being pulled back and forth reminds me of a game I learned while living in Hartford. It was a jump rope game called, Double-Dutch. Two people hold two jump ropes in their hands and turn each rope toward the other. The jumper would rock back and forth, waiting for an opening to jump in without disturbing the rhythm. It took some doing, but eventually my sister Debbie and I mastered it! Playing Double-Dutch was one of our favorite pastimes and the girls in the neighborhood welcomed us with open arms.

We were glad to be back with mom; however, we quickly began to see how much of a drinker she was. She drank every day, sometimes all day. I don't remember how long we were in Hartford. My mother got really drunk one evening and dragged me and Debbie downstairs to the pay phone on the corner. She had a pocket full of dimes that she was putting in. She dialed a number and when the man answered, she began to yell and curse. After a while, he would hang up on her, but she would call him right back. This went on until she ran out of coins.

We would later find out that the man she was calling was my father. That behavior from mom let my father know where we were. Soon after, we were heading back to Florida.

"The Florida skies are like no other, with cloud formations that are awesome! Even when it rains, the sun shines through the drops."

– Connie Letang

CHAPTER SEVEN

Sunshine Again

If memory serves me correctly, we were back at Miss Alice's house in Delray. But that wouldn't last long.

"Please don't take the girls," we heard Miss Alice say.

The questions started swirling inside me again. What is happening? Are we leaving? My father was leaving Miss Alice and taking us away. By this time, I was five or six years old. I'm not sure why we were leaving, where we were going, what my dad was thinking, why he didn't listen to Miss Alice's pleas not to take us. What I do know is that we were on the move, again.

Daytona Beach, Florida. Home to the World's Most Famous Beach. Home of Mary McLeod Bethune and Bethune-Cookman College as it was called at that time. This was going to be our new home. We moved in an area called Madison Heights. My father rented a house from a man named Mr. Sheppard, and the three of us – dad, myself, and my sister moved in. The house was nice. It had been beautifully kept including the landscaping. We settled down to the business of living once again without my mother.

Christmas was approaching and I wasn't thrilled about it until my mother decided to reconcile with my father! Oh, happy day! Dad told us she was coming, and we were excited! The day finally came when mother arrived in Daytona. I don't remember whether she arrived in a cab, or my dad picked her up but all I know is I had my mother back!!

Things were going well for a while. We were so happy to have her back! We were attending Lambert's Temple COGIC and she started going to church with us. It finally felt like we had a real family. I had a mama in the house! It was nice coming home from school and having her there. She was short and feisty, and she read a lot.

She would curl up on the sofa for hours reading romance novels. Aside from that, she spent an awful long time in the bathroom. *"What in the world could she be doing in there?"* I always wondered. It wasn't too long before I would discover the answer. I don't know what made me look but hidden in the tank of the toilet was a liquor bottle! She had started drinking again.

Shortly after that, the arguments between she and my dad resurfaced. Loud, mean words would fly between them. A lady at the church got up during service and proclaimed before the whole church to my mother, "God is saying you are still smoking and drinking"

Mama was so mad and when we got home, she and daddy argued about that. Mama angrily said, "she had no right to do that! I am never going back there!"

Daddy wasn't helping. It was as if he was agreeing with how that lady approached mama. They argued back and forth, and mama called him "a sorry sack of bones" for not defending her. Debbie and I listened from our bedroom. We didn't know what to do. It was clear things were not going well between them. Would they be able to work things out? It was Christmas for heaven's sake.

"God, please don't let her leave again!" I prayed.

"The holiday season is a perfect time to reflect on our blessings and seek ways to make life better for those around us."

– Anonymous

CHAPTER EIGHT

Merry Christmas

Christmas was fast approaching. Debbie and I decorated the tree while mom read her books. We hung lights and ornaments on a white artificial tree. It was beautiful. This was the best time ever! Things seemed to have settled down between mom and daddy. I thought they would be okay. I surely prayed so. Debbie and I were worried because we didn't want her to go away again.

We made it to Christmas eve before the bottom fell out. Dad and Mom were arguing again. It wasn't working between them. Mom had enough of whatever was going on. We heard her tell dad, "I'm leaving after Christmas and I'm not taking the girls with me."

Debbie and I were dumfounded, and we began to cry. Debbie whispered to me, "this time we are going with her."

"How?" I asked, with tears streaming down my face. "She said she not taking us."

"Then we will sneak in the cab and then sneak on the bus! She's not leaving us!" Debbie countered. It sounded like a good plan to me. I agreed. Then she calmly told me, "Pack some clothes."

Christmas morning was very gloomy. I hardly remember any gifts. I was too heartbroken knowing that immediately after Christmas and before my seventh birthday, Mom would be gone. Debbie and I spent the day in our room. It didn't feel much like Christmas at all. We were heartbroken. We were hoping that Mama changed her mind and was going to stay after all. We tried to keep close watch on her every move. We were on watch, and ready to sneak in the cab when Mom got ready to leave. That night I don't think either one of us slept very much. The night seemed like an eternity, but the day finally came, and Debbie and I were ready to put our plan into action.

Mama finally told us that she would be leaving. "Girls, I have to go. I'm sorry but you girls can't go with me. You have to stay here with your dad." I don't remember too much after that except crying.

Debbie and I were ready. As soon as she went outside to get in the cab, we would sneak in the backseat then sneak on the bus. It was a great plan except, she didn't call for a cab! Daddy was taking her.

"Elizabeth," he called, "Let's go!" This is *not* what is supposed to happen!! This is not the plan. "Deborah, Regina, get in the car!" Daddy yelled.

We didn't know what to do. How were we going to get on that bus? We cried all the way to the Greyhound bus station. Our mother was leaving again returning north to Hartford. *"Why God? What did we do wrong?"* I thought.

We arrived at the station, and we all got out of the car. Mom grabbed her bags and headed to the ticket counter. We waited with dad outside. Finally, she came out with her ticket in hand. She hugged us, kissed our tear-stained faces, and boarded the bus.

This is not happening. This is not happening! How could she just leave us like that? I was sobbing.

"Get in the car!" Daddy yelled, and as much as we wanted to run after her and somehow get on that bus, we got in the car. He pulled off before the bus left and headed back home. That would be the last time I would see her face until 21 years later.

The whole ordeal felt unreal. It felt like we were moving in slow motion. Knowing that we would return home without her was unbearable. It was the longest ride of our lives. We cried the whole way and daddy never said a word. I got introduced to new cousins named neglect, abandonment, and rejection. From that moment on, I felt insignificant. Some *Merry* Christmas.

> *"Every great dream begins with a dreamer. Always remember, you have within you the strength, the patience, and the passion to reach for the stars to change the world."*
>
> *– Harriet Tubman*

CHAPTER NINE

On the Move, Again

Not long after mama left, we moved out of Mr. Sheppard's house. It was alright though because the memory of her being there was too much, at least for my tiny heart. For months following, I just couldn't believe she was gone. I kept waiting for her to come back and steal us again. I would look out of the windows for her. The next knock on the door would be her. I held my breath every day, hoping that she would show up. I would hope on any given day, when I came home from school, she would be there. To my knowledge, she never attempted to kidnap us again.

The church we attended, and my father ministered in, had a room on the second floor. I suppose that it had once been used for office space. This is where we moved to. It was small and cramped. Debbie and I shared a regular bed on one side of the room and daddy slept in a twin bed on the other side. The church kitchen and bathrooms were downstairs.

It was creepy living there. I remember one time while we were there, someone died, and they held the funeral service there. Like they used to do back in the day, the body was left in the church overnight following the wake service. Because the kitchen and bathrooms were downstairs, we would have to go downstairs to use the bathroom, near the dead body in the casket! I would beg Debbie to go with me. "Please come with me," I would say.

"Stop being a baby and go pee girl" she would say. I would ease down those stairs as if the dead person would rise and get me. Talk about peeing fast!

Debbie always seemed to be in a mood, and I didn't understand why at the time. I won't say she was mean, but she was. She always seemed bothered by me, and for me, with mama gone, she was all I had. You would think we would be closer since we both were hurting but she was processing her pain differently. Later in life, I would find out some of what she was dealing with. Then I understood her perpetual mood.

So once again, we settled into our new life and new living arrangements. Daddy had become a truck driver and was often out of town. We would stay with various people from our church when he was away. It became our way of life. I didn't mind. Most of the people we would stay with, were women from the church. They took good care of us while he was away.

My favorite people to stay with were the Pastor of our church, Pastor Lambert, and Lady Lambert! She was so nice to Debbie and me. She would take us everywhere she went. I remember her making brown paper gift bags for Christmas. They would always have an orange, an apple, hard Christmas candy and nuts. I was always sad when we had to leave her home.

We went to school and attended church of course. We didn't have many friends outside of the few we had at school. Life was tough on us primarily because Debbie and I missed our mama so bad. Even though Debbie and I missed her, we didn't talk about it. I don't know why. We were becoming numb to what was happening around us. The days were mundane at best, and we specialized in settling into what our lives could become.

Just as we were accepting the possibility of never seeing or hearing from our mom, a big box came in the mail. It was from Mama! The return address said "Elizabeth Hopkins, Hartford, Connecticut." The box was for me and Debbie! We were so excited! Did this mean she would come back after all? We ripped that box open to find the prettiest clothes we'd ever seen! These were some *up North* style clothes. Nobody in Florida was wearing anything like the dresses and outfits in that box! There were cute print dresses, tops with matching slacks along with black patent leather shoes. She had even put stockings in there and we weren't wearing stockings then!

There was a note in the box. "Hi girls. I wanted to send you all a few things. Love, mama."

Over the next few months, she would send several boxes of clothes based on the season. We looked forward to receiving those boxes whenever they came. It was like having a small piece of mama with us. It was exciting like waking up on Christmas morning opening gifts! We lived for those boxes.

After a while, the boxes arrived irregularly and eventually stopped coming. And just like that, the connection to mama ended - again.

"The only impossible journey is the one you never begin."
– Tony Robbins

CHAPTER TEN

New Day

I was nine when daddy remarried, and we moved into a larger place. The house wasn't anything fancy, but it was larger than the place we had previously lived. There were three bedrooms which was more than enough for our now growing family. The house was very strangely built with two sides divided in the middle by the bathroom. I didn't like it neither did Debbie, but children seldom have a say in such adult decisions.

My stepmother, Annie Mae, had three boys from a previous marriage: Tony age five, Donnell age four, and the baby Bernard, who was one. We instantly went from two children to five. I will not lie. I wasn't happy with this new formed family. Suddenly, we were told that Daddy was going to marry her. Before we met her in person, Daddy gave us a picture. That's it.

Debbie asked me simply, "what you gone call her?"

I inquired sarcastically, "what's her name?"

"Annie Mae," Debbie responded.

"Then, that's what I will call her."

For nine years of my life, it was always Debbie and me. But over time, I began to love and care for my brothers. They were after all, children in a new space just like Debbie and I, and they had no say so in the marriage or this new family either. Besides, they were good boys. I really took to the baby boy, Bernard. He was so innocent and happy! They stopped being my stepbrothers. They were, and still are, my brothers! Having this new family, however, did not stop my heart from longing for my mother. Even though our time together had not been long, she was still *MY* mother and I missed her so much.

Outside of school, church, home and taking care of the boys, life was mundane. We weren't allowed to associate with other children. Daddy was extremely private. What happened in our house, stayed in our house. Period! But there was five of us then and the boys occupied much of that emptiness - especially Bernard. He was so cute. He gave me a reason to smile.

Debbie and I went about our way doing what we were told to do. In addition to looking after the boys, going to school and church, there was washing and ironing clothes, washing dishes, and keeping the house clean. I felt like the maid and the nanny. I decided I would keep my head down and not get in any trouble but Debbie, was another story for another book!

Time went on and another baby boy named Lawrence was born. Debbie took to him like he was hers! Since the family was growing, we moved, again, into an even larger house. The house was on a street called Tomoka Road. Nothing remarkable except it was an older home with a huge yard with an orange tree and plum trees. It had a screened in front porch where me and the boys would play sometime. Directly across the street lived a lady name Miss Freda. She lived there with her mother. I don't know what made us start playing this game, but we knew Miss Freda would sit on her front porch all the time and we thought it would be fun to aggravate her while she did.

So, we would call out to her, "Hey Fredadita!" Then we would duck so she couldn't see us.

One day she walked across the street and angrily demanded, "Stop playing with me before I tell your parents!"

We were so scared; we never played that game again. During this time Debbie was having a hard time. She began running away from home often. Daddy would find her, usually at a classmate's house, and bring her back. A belt on her backside didn't stop her from running. I attributed it to her missing our mama. I would not find out what was really happening with her until we were grown. Although she was four years older, I always felt like the oldest. I'm not sure why, but my brain worked differently than most kids my age. I was a thinker. I never took anything at face value. I had to flip it over, turn it around, flip it again before I was satisfied.

I remember telling Debbie one time, after she had run away and daddy found her, brought her home and beat her with a belt, "You got to just lay low, do what you're told, and you won't keep getting in trouble."

She would say, "Shut-up! You don't know nothing Miss Goody-two-shoes!"

I wasn't trying to be a goody-two-shoes, I feared if she didn't behave, they might send her away and I couldn't bear losing my mama and my sister. She was all I had. Eventually what I feared the most happened. Debbie was sent to live with my stepmother's mother, Villa in a small North Florida city called Jasper.

I remember that day so clearly. My parents had taken Debbie somewhere. I don't know where. It was a school day so they must have taken her out of school early. The car pulled up in the yard, I went to the bedroom. The three of them came into the house.

Daddy was yelling at Debbie saying, "you're not going to ruin my reputation."

Debbie was crying. She walked to the bedroom and started packing a suitcase.

"Wait, where are you going?" I asked her but she wouldn't answer me. "Debbie what's wrong? What happened? What did you do?" She never answered me.

"Let's go," daddy commanded!

She was crying when she got in the car, and they drove away. I was in my room crying my eyes out. I had no idea what was happening, and nobody bothered to tell me. All I know is MY SISTER WAS GONE! JUST LIKE MY MAMA! That day changed my heart. I was wounded yet again. I felt abandoned - again. I was invisible - again. I was angry. He took my sister away and ran my mama away! It was like he didn't like us or something. I did not understand. Why were these things happening to me, to Debbie? Did he resent us like he resented our mother? Why didn't he just leave us with Auntie?

I was heartbroken. The one person that tied me to our mother, was gone. She wasn't allowed to come back home. It would be years before I would find out what was so terrible that they would send her away. At 15, she had been raped by a teacher at school. She told daddy and he didn't believe her. She was banished from our home.

"Life is either a daring adventure or nothing at all."
– Helen Keller

CHAPTER ELEVEN

Here We Go Again

Not long after Debbie was sent away, we moved again. My parents were able to buy an even larger place, and this would be the last home I would live in with the family. We lived in a subdivision of Daytona Beach affectionately called Skeeter Creek. It derived its name because of new homes being built in an area that was plagued by mosquitoes! The house had four bedrooms and two bathrooms I had my own room, and the two oldest boys shared a room, while the two youngest boys shared another room.

Shortly after we moved in, daddy put up a chain-link fence around the property. I will never forget the words he said when he was done. "Nobody in, nobody out." Daddy did not want people in our business. We could not have friends at our house. And we weren't allowed to go to anybody else's house. Period.

In the blue and white house across the street from us lived an older couple caring for their two granddaughters, Yolonda and her sister Linda, who I became friends with. Yolonda was the oldest of the two and a year younger than me. She was nice, extremely cute, and quite popular unlike me. We went to the same school, Mainland Senior High School, home of the Buccaneers!

Even though we weren't supposed to have people in the house, Yolonda would come over especially during the summer months. My stepmother would be at work, daddy would be on the road and her grandparents worked, so we visited each other's houses! We always kept up with the time so we wouldn't get caught. We would watch the traffic between the houses for daddy's 18-wheeler, so we knew when to part ways. One day, we got so wrapped up in listening to music and Yolonda braiding my hair, that we didn't see or hear the truck until it was in front of my house.

Yolonda took off running towards the back patio and jumped that doggone fence into my classmate Cookie Crafton's yard! She walked the whole way around the subdivision so Daddy couldn't tell that she came from our house. We laughed about that for years! We lost touch after high school but were briefly reunited. Sadly, Yolonda passed away not long after we met each other as adults.

I was never an unruly or disrespectful child, but I was broken. I spent most of my time to myself (after my chores of course and taking care of the boys). I loved to read, and I, like my mom, read often. My days were spent mostly in my room either reading or listening to music on the transistor radio (that I wasn't supposed to have). A transistor radio was a small handheld portable device that used batteries to operate. At the time, it only had AM frequency. I don't know how I came to own it. I may have gotten it from Yolonda. I kept it hidden so that I could listen to music when Daddy wasn't home or late at night when he was asleep. I never got caught with it!

Since my father was a pastor, we heard his command often, "no devil music will be played in my house!" I recall borrowing a

Motown album from Cookie. I kept it hidden under my mattress. I came home from school one day and the album was on my bed, broken in pieces. Daddy found it because they bought me a new mattress. I got a mouthful of bad girl admonishment that day. I wanted to die when I had to tell Cookie her album was gone.

I told daddy that the album didn't belong to me. He angrily said, "I don't care who it belongs to. It's not supposed to be in my house."

As I grew older, my mother became a distant memory and so did Debbie. The phrase out of sight, out of mind is a real thing. The more time passed, the less I allowed myself to think about either of them. I learned how to push the thought of them deep down inside. The only tangible thing I had was my hurt, sorrow, and a broken heart. Debbie was not mentioned at least where I could hear. It was as if she never existed. Just like mama.

I loved music! I started singing in church when I was quite young. Because I was so short, they would stand me in a chair so people could see me! I joined the glee club at school when I was in the eleventh grade. Music had a way of transporting me out of the space I was in and carried me into a whole different world. It was as if each note I sang lifted me and moved me to a different time and place. If I could have had my way, I would have lived in the choir room. Miss Chevalier was our music teacher. She was tough, but I loved her! She took an interest in my ability to sing and was teaching me to read music. She even took me to a sight-reading competition once. I didn't make it.

That year she put on the musical "Oklahoma" and wanted to give me a part. I told her I couldn't stay after school for rehearsals. I had to get home to be there when my brothers came home. She asked me if she could come to my house and speak to my parents. I asked her not to. I felt some kind of way having to explain that if she asked them to allow me to perform, she would get me in trouble.

I didn't get to do many after school functions because I was the eldest and I had to get straight home after school to look after my brothers. But whenever there was an assembly during school hours and the choir had to sing, man oh man, I was in there many times as the soloist. Unlike other kids, school was my solace, my haven, my distraction from all the things that were breaking my heart. Yes, school was where I could escape.

"All mankind is divided into three classes: those that are immovable, those that are movable, and those that move."

– Benjamin Franklin

CHAPTER TWELVE

It's Almost Time

Before my eleventh-grade year ended, there was another baby boy born. He was named Ronnie. I don't know if there was not enough room in my parents' room or what, but his crib was placed in my room. I wasn't happy about getting up in the middle of the night to feed him or change him, but I realized like me, he wasn't to blame. He was a baby. His being in my room was a choice someone else made. Like the choice my mother made wasn't my fault.

So, I loved him and took great care of him. For the first year of his life, he thought I was his mother. He cried more for me than he did for his actual mom. He went everywhere with me. On senior sneak day, I took him to school. He was always with me. I was sad and Ronnie made me happy.

Out of all the Christmases that had come and gone since that fateful Christmas with my mother, one of the ones that stand out was my baby brother Ronnie's first one. It stands out not because of gifts I received or decorations we put up but because of Ronnie. The lights on the Christmas tree fascinated him as he scooted around in his walker. Like a speeding car, he rolled over to that tree and before I could stop him, he reached out and grabbed one of the branches and pulled that tree over on top of himself! I noticed him first because I always had an eye on him.

He was completely covered by that tree and crying his little heart out! I rushed over, lifted the tree off him, and picked him up to make sure that he was okay! As I checked his little body to assure he was all right, I comforted him, "Oh, my goodness! Shhhhhh, poor baby, you're ok. Shhhhhh, it's okay. I got you."

After I was sure he wasn't seriously injured, and after he quieted down, I put him back in his walker and off he went as if nothing had happened. Oh, the pure innocence of children!

One of the joys I did experience at Christmas time in Daytona was when we would visit a display presented each year by a family called The Chestnuts. The display had a life-size mechanical Santa and Mrs. Claus, and a stable with animals, wise men, and of course a baby Jesus. The house had so many lights, it lit up the whole neighborhood! I don't remember too much more about Christmas from my childhood; but the memory of that house still makes me smile. Maybe somewhere tucked in the recesses of my mind, other memories reside and hopefully - if they ever come back - they will be good ones.

"It takes courage to grow up and become who you really are."

– E.E. Cummings

CHAPTER THIRTEEN

Sir, Yes Sir!

It was 1974 and I was preparing to graduate from high school! There was nothing remarkable about this time. No senior packet, no class ring, no yearbook, no senior prom, no Spring social. Nothing. Outside of the glee club, I wasn't involved in any other school activities. I still felt invisible. Since my birthday falls in January, I was already eighteen, according to the law, I was an adult.

I had to make some decisions about where my life was headed. I needed to decide if I would go to college or get a job. I always wanted to attend Bethune-Cookman College. I grew up in the city where Mary McCleod Bethune started the school! Music would have been my major, since I have a nice singing voice. But that would mean staying at home because Daddy said I could not live on campus. Getting a job would also mean staying home so I didn't want that either.

My parents never had a conversation with me about my future. Ever. A relationship with my father was nonexistent. He was my father. I was his daughter. Period. We lived under the same roof, but we never talked. About anything not even about his childhood. This was a pivotal moment that changed the trajectory of my life. I was so broken and sad yet seeking out my mother for some type of help or respite never crossed my mind. If it did, I suppressed it. She was a distant memory. She was not allowed to occupy space in my head and certainly not in my heart. My crying, longing, yearning for her was over. Whatever questions I may have had no longer required answers. She didn't come back for me, she never wrote, she never called. For me it was a done deal.

One day during school, recruiters from different branches of the military came to recruit those who were interested, or whomever they could convince to enlist. When they came, they issued military aptitude tests to all the students that wanted to take them.

The possibility of leaving home and being on my own was scary. I had no life skills and had no clue where I would go or how I would take care of myself. I just knew I was ready to leave. I began to think about going into the military. I wanted to join the Air Force so when they offered the test, I took it. My thinking was that joining the military would help me get established as a young adult, gain independence, and be in a safe space. I took the test, which was administered for all the branches of the military. I wanted more than anything to enter the Air Force, but I missed their requirements by six points!

The recruiter said, "you can take it again in six months." I didn't have six months. It was close to graduation day; and I needed a sure plan, or I would not have anywhere to go. I wanted out of that house and out of Daytona and if this didn't work, I would be stuck in a house with people that didn't like me.

I was contacted by the Coast Guard shortly thereafter. I scored high enough for them and they wanted to know if they could come speak to me. I said, "Absolutely, but it would have to be during school hours."

They agreed.

The recruiters came to the school and talked to me about all the benefits one would receive joining The Guard. It sounded good to me. I signed up and was sworn in. I would be graduating on June 6, 1974 and would leave for basic training in Cape May, New Jersey on June 14th, eight days later. I was nervously excited and scared. I knew my father was not going to approve, but I didn't care. I was in total survival mode and this decision was about me and no one else. I was eighteen, sworn in, and there would be nothing he could do about it.

The day came when the officers had to bring my orders to report to the recruiting station in Jacksonville, Florida and then on to New Jersey. School was out so they had to come to the house! Oh, my goodness; I was a bundle of nerves! The day the officers arrived at the house; daddy was sitting in the living room watching television. The front door was open but the screen door, which was attached to it, was locked. I saw their car pull up from my bedroom window. Since I knew they were coming, I hid out in my room. I deliberately did not tell daddy, though it wouldn't have mattered, and it wasn't negotiable.

Two handsome fellows in white uniforms were coming in the gate. The gate that my daddy demanded, "no one in, no one out."

I heard daddy yell as he made his way to the door, "Who is that?' I swallowed hard and stepped into the hallway as he asked, "May I help you?"

One of the officers identified himself and said, "is this the home of Kerrie Hopkins?"

"Yes," my father answered.

"Sir, may we come in?" The officer inquired as he removed his hat.

My father was eyeing them in total confusion. I was watching from the hallway.

Finally, he said, "come on in." The two officers stepped into the house. My father turned his head towards the bedrooms and yelled, "Regina!"

"Yes sir." I replied.

"Come here." He demanded.

I appeared in the living room. The officers smiled at me. I felt empowered! I was making decisions about my life and there was nothing anyone could do about it.

My daddy was not pleased at all! "What is going on here?"

For the first time in my life, I was proud to give him an answer. "I joined the Coast Guard."

He was livid. He looked at me in total disbelief. His head turned to one side, hand on his hip. "You did what?"

I proudly said, "I joined the Coast Guard."

My father being the great orator that he was, was speechless for a moment. Then he said, "You didn't ask me if you could do that. Absolutely not!" Before I could say anything, he spoke to the officers. "My daughter does not have my permission to go in no Coast Guard!"

One of the officers gently informed my father, "Sir, with all due respect, she is eighteen years old. The law says she is an adult.

She has taken the oath to protect and defend, she's been sworn in, and she now belongs to the United States Coast Guard. There is absolutely nothing you can do about it and if you try to interfere, you can and will be arrested."

I had never seen my daddy so outdone. He was fuming. One of the officers turned and handed me an envelope.

"Seaman Apprentice Hopkins, these are your orders. You are to report to The Coast Guard Recruiting Office in Jacksonville, Florida on June 14, 1974, by way of Greyhound Bus Lines. You will find your ticket inside this package. Once you arrive in Jacksonville, you will be given a plane ticket to Philadelphia, PA. There is a bus from the base that will pick you up and you will be transported to your basic training station at Cape May, New Jersey. Do you understand?"

I knew my life was going to dramatically change as I raised my right hand and slowly brought it towards my face, thumb tucked under, and my remaining fingers rested just above my brow line in salute.

"Sir, yes sir!" And with that, the officers left. Daddy never said another word about it. The rest of the family stayed in their room. And that was that. I was preparing to step out into the world, and I still had not seen or heard from Debbie.

"*Bravery is being the only one who knows you're afraid.*"

– Franklin P. Jones

CHAPTER FOURTEEN

New Beginnings

I was starting a brand-new life away from the place I had known for twelve years. It was scary but I would not be traveling alone. My friend from school, Veronica Jones, who also lived in my neighborhood was going too! We enlisted under the buddy system. We were the first Black females to be recruited and enlisted from Florida at that time!

The day I left home my stepmother took me to the bus along with my brothers. The baby, who had spent the first year or so in my room, had a fit as I was boarding that bus. It broke my heart. I imagined he felt the same way I felt the day my mama stepped on her Greyhound bus years before. He was crying and so was I. I hugged him as hard as I could and kissed his little face. I hugged my stepmom and thanked her, and Veronica and I boarded.

The bus pulled away from the station and we were on our way. Our first time away from home. Two young ladies as green as the grass! Meaning we didn't know what to expect! We were excited to see what lied ahead. We talked about sticking together, making a career in the military, rising in the ranks and all the places we would travel to. Maybe we would get to go overseas, Japan, Germany, France and then be able to retire at 38 years old with 20 years of service and still be young enough to enjoy life! It was a good, solid plan.

The ride to Jacksonville, wasn't bad and soon we were pulling into the station. Once we got off the bus, we spotted a uniformed officer who was there to pick us up. He was a tall, handsome young man with chocolate skin. His uniform was nice and crisp, and he had a beautiful smile. I thought to myself, *"wow he is good looking."* He introduced himself and loaded our bags as we got in the car.

He took us to our hotel where we would stay for the night before leaving for Philadelphia the next evening. We checked into the hotel and went to our room. He offered to show us around town. Veronica didn't want to go but I did. So, I left with him. He stopped by the recruiting building where he worked. It was in a high-rise, and he wanted to show me the view from his office. You could see a line of tall, beautifully lit buildings. I was captivated by the splendor of it all.

I was a young naïve girl, away from home for the first time. I was easy pickings. When it became obvious that this was the only stop we would be making, I knew I had made a mistake. Suddenly, he kissed me. I was attracted to him, so I didn't stop him. I didn't stop him when he started to undress me. I was frozen inside my own mind. I knew this was not what I came here for, but I could not say a word. I felt powerless and afraid. I didn't say anything until the pain of him trying to penetrate me hurt so bad that I yelled, "STOP! You're hurting me!"

He tried to convince me that it would be okay.

I screamed, "NO! Please take me back to the hotel."

He was angry. "Put your clothes on and let's go!"

On the ride back to the hotel, there was silence in the car. He dropped me off and left. I was so ashamed that I never spoke about it until now. It was my fault. I blamed myself for even getting in the car with him. I blamed myself for not having the courage to stop him at the first kiss. I was too ashamed to even tell Veronica what happened. It was another incident in my life that I would stuff deep inside of me.

The next day, he picked us up, acted like nothing happened between us, gave us our plane tickets, and dropped us at the airport. I was so excited about what was ahead of me that I didn't think about that night. I decided it would be something else I would suppress. Between the excitement of arriving and sexual assault, I don't even remember calling home to say I made it to Jacksonville.

While writing this, I decided to walk-through that painful, shameful time in my life and it made me realize, unlike all the other times that I had no voice – that time - I spoke up! I used my voice to say STOP! I took back my power and would not allow him to continue to hurt me! Quietly and unnoticed by me, his predatory behavior made my voice arise.

Our first plane ride was exhilarating and indescribable. It was a little scary especially travelling at night! I didn't know what turbulence was, but I soon found out. We kept hitting pockets of air that would cause the plane to suddenly drop making us feel like we were on a roller coaster! Veronica and I would hold hands and squeeze tight! I don't remember having a lot of conversation, with all that turbulence, we just wanted to see land safely and soon. This would be my first experience with ears popping aboard an aircraft as well. I didn't know then the trick to keeping my ears open was to chew gum! That part was not fun. But all in all, it was not a bad journey.

The plane finally landed in Philadelphia, and I was glad we were out of the air and back on land. We were met at the airport by this short, scruffy looking Caucasian fellow from the base. He wasn't only there for Veronica and me, he was picking up several young people heading to that base! He marched us outside to this huge grey gloomy looking bus that looked like we were being carted off to a prison! Once we boarded, he made an announcement over the intercom.

"Hello, we are headed to the United States Coast Guard Basic Training Station. There will be no talking. Is that understood?"

"Sir, yes sir" we all said in concert.

"Good."

He climbed in the driver's seat, and we pulled off. That was the scariest hour or so long ride into the night.

"We cannot direct the wind, but we can adjust the sails."
– Dolly Parton

CHAPTER FIFTEEN

It's All About Me

We finally arrived in the dead of night to the base. To me it was a dreary looking place surrounded by water. It reminded me of Alcatraz. I wondered why it was situated like that. Did they think we would try to escape? The driver stopped at the security gate, he and the guard exchanged pleasantries before he raised the arm on the gate, and we drove through.

Once he stopped in front of one of the buildings, we exited the bus, and retrieved our suitcases, and were escorted into the barracks. There were other girls already there and once this person walked in; his shoes made a sound on the floor like shoes with metal taps on them.

Someone yelled, "attention in the squad bay!" All the girls stood at attention and saluted as he walked by.

He returned the salute and said, "at ease."

He walked us all in and assigned us to bunks. As we were walking in, I noticed that the room was split by an aisle and bunk beds were on both sides. I would later learn that we were two different companies sharing the squad bay. Twenty girls on either side of the aisle. They did not make eye contact as we passed.

The floors shined like glass. I quickly learned that we had to keep them that way! We were instructed to put our things in the lockers that were at the head of the bunk and get some sleep. He would be back in the morning.

"Lights out," he yelled as he made his exit. The lights went off while we were still putting our things away leaving us in the dark.

I managed to get myself into bed and lay there feeling excited and scared at the same time. I didn't think about anybody, not Mama, not Daddy, not Debbie. They were as distant to me in this moment as that bus ride had been from Philly. This moment sealed my heart regarding what anybody else wanted from me. I was on my own and everything was about my survival.

I had no idea what this journey had in store for me, but I had no time to waste thinking about or missing anyone. They weren't thinking about or missing me. To hell with all of them! Except the boys and my baby brother. I missed them.

It was all about me. It was all about what I wanted and needed. Nobody else would hurt me. I put the abandonment, neglect, and rejection issues aside. I was quiet and guarded. I simply wanted to get through basic training and get to living this military life while Uncle Sam took care of me as I grew up. That's it. That's all.

Training lasted for about three months. I had issues with some of the other young ladies in the squad bay particularly with the other company that we shared space with. We were all assigned different chores to keep the barracks clean. There would be arguments among the girls as to which company cleaned what, when, and so on. The girls got into a screaming match one

Saturday over who would wax the floor. We couldn't agree, so neither side did it. We cleaned everything else.

When the Company Commander found out about the bickering amongst us, he had the men smear toothpaste all over the mirrors in the bathroom (the head as it was called) and throw buckets of sand on top of it! They also scuffed up the floors that had not been waxed. The Commander entered the barracks, and someone yelled. "Attention in the squad bay." We all stopped cleaning and stood at attention. I can still hear those shoes on the floor.

He finally spoke, "At ease." He looked at us as he walked and talked saying, "Since you ladies can't' seem to figure out who does what, your leave for today has been cancelled. I want this place spit shined. I better not find one grain of sand in that bathroom. You will learn to get along, work together, and become a team. Is that understood ladies?"

We all responded in concert, "Sir, yes sir!"

"As you were." And with that he exited the barracks.

I was not involved in this foolishness but I along with the others, paid the price. So, I decided to see if we could make peace for the duration of the time we had left together. I talked it over with them and we worked it out. I still wanted to punch a couple of people though.

Training consisted of taking classes, learning the history of the Guard, swimming classes, as well as learning how to handle a weapon. We trained on the M-16 Rifle as well as the 45 semi-automatic pistols. We learned how to break it down, clean it and put it back together. In addition, we had daily calisthenics. We would rise early for our morning run. We had to get in formation, run in formation, and stay in formation. Because I was the shortest in my company it was hard to keep up. Every day, I was the last to make the stretch in front of the brass and my company would have to run an extra lap! I felt so bad that they all had to suffer because of me.

I recall one morning while on the run, I began to fall behind. Suddenly, my feet left the ground! Two guys picked me up and carried me around that track. Just as we got near the commanders, they put me down! That day at least, they did not have to run an extra lap.

We needed a plan. We finally figured out a strategy. They put me in front and let me set the pace! It worked! After all those extra laps, I lost quite a bit of weight. When I arrived at the base, I was a size 16. By the time, I graduated, I had to be reissued new uniforms in a size eight!

Finally, graduation day came. Veronica had graduated a week before me because I had failed a weekly progress test. I can't remember if my parents even came which means they didn't. I met the mother of one of the young men that was in my company, during the graduation ceremony. Her name was Charlotte. She congratulated me and it made me feel proud of my accomplishment. I didn't know it at the time, but she would later become my mother in-law.

"When disappointment festers in our soul, it leads to discouragement."

– Joyce Meyer

CHAPTER SIXTEEN

Just Like That

After graduating from basic training, I was sent to The Coast Guard Aviation Training Center in Mobile, Alabama. But before I reported, I did go home to Daytona for a visit. I was so trim that my stepmother didn't recognize me in my uniform. I was happy to see my brothers! I spent a few days there and then reported to base.

When the cab pulled up to the guard gate, I showed my identification, and we were let through the gate. The base was beautiful. There were several buildings surrounded by trees and sidewalks. To the left sat the building where the Commanding Officer's office was. As we drove farther in, I saw the Officer's Club, the Enlisted Men's Club, the Commissary and around the bend to my right, was the hanger that housed the Coast Guard helicopters. This base is a training station that teaches the Seaman Apprentice's to fly helicopters and learn search and rescue. Once again, I made history as one of two females ever stationed aboard the base and the first African American female in the history of that base. That was August of 1974.

An incredibly attractive Black male met me in front of the building I was reporting to. He helped me with my bags and escorted me to my quarters. There, I met Seaman Apprentice, Julie Lakey. She was from Mountain Home, Arkansas and she was as country as they came! She spoke with a southern twang, didn't wear makeup and if not for the uniform, would never dress up! She had the sweetest disposition which made it easy for us to bond.

We would share quarters together on the first floor of the three-story barracks which meant the guys who were already bunking on that floor, had to move up to the second and third level. The barracks instantly became coed. They were not happy. We could not be on the same floor for any reason at any time! There would be no fraternizing. Whenever Julie or I wanted to watch TV, which was on the second floor, they had to clear the entire floor the whole time we were there! Whew!

When we would walk into the room, we would get looks and hear sighs as they would begin to leave the space. We wanted to be a part of the team! They didn't like us being there at all.

News got out that there were two females stationed aboard the base and the next thing we knew; a news station came out and interviewed us! That was my first appearance on television; and it was cool!

Julie and I spent our time together on and off base getting to know our duties as well as the city. Some weekends, we would beg the guys to take us to the malls or to the beaches. Occasionally, we would spend time in the Enlisted Men's Club. Everything was going great, and I was having a blast!

Since we arrived straight from bootcamp, we were at the bottom of the totem pole as far as our duties. My recruiter specifically told me I would be going to Yeoman School (fancy for secretary) from basic training. That was a lie. Instead of wearing dress blues, we put on our navy-blue cargo pants and, chambray shirt and commenced to cleaning the base, painting, and working in the mess hall among other duties. I was disappointed but not deterred. I would request to go to school.

It wasn't too long before I got my heart broken. A guy in personnel, who received and processed my records, knew what I looked like. I was cute! He showed some of the guys my picture, and a bet was wagered to see which one of them would get to me first. Of course, I didn't know this.

The nice gentleman who had met me my first day would show me around the base. Since Julie nor I had a car, he would also show me about town. We became fast friends and I enjoyed hanging out with him. Eventually he told me about the bet and advised me to be careful with the other guys. I was appalled! He would be the only person I trusted. Everybody else was suspect. We spent time together often, going to the movies or hanging out at the club on the base. Church was nowhere on my mind even though I was a preacher's kid. I was on my own and living my life.

I was settling into military life and having a blast. I tried to drink alcohol, but it made me sick on the stomach and too tipsy. It didn't take me long to walk away from that. I never wanted to not be in control of where I was and wake up in a strange place; and alcohol was the drug of choice for my mother. I didn't want to be anything like her.

I began to spend more time with the greeter. I liked him. He liked me. Or so I thought. He was pleasant and easy to be around. Of course, he was much older. He made me laugh and had a bright smile. I loved to hear him laugh. It was infectious. It would not be long before we were in a relationship. It was great. He was great.

I was in love. I had the career I wanted. Life was good, no, life was great! If my mama, sister, daddy, or any of the family, came across my mind, I would tuck them all so far back in my mind that I almost forgot they even existed!

News got around quickly that I was in a relationship with the greeter and then it happened. I discovered, by accident, that not only was he the one who made the bet, but he was also married. I was crushed, humiliated, and embarrassed. Once again, someone had ripped out my heart.

And just like that, it was over. I found the strength even with a broken heart, to end it.

"Problems are inevitable. Misery is a choice."

– Ann Landers

CHAPTER SEVENTEEN

Misery Does Love Company

To say I was a miserable wreck was an understatement. I was devastated and to add insult to injury, I was assigned to work with the one who betrayed me. He was my superior! He didn't want to break things off and when I did, he made my life a living hell on the base. I couldn't complain because, I was a consenting adult.

Eventually, I would go to the Commanding Officer requesting a transfer to another base. Each time, it was denied. It seemed that the whole world was against me. So, I j did my assigned work and tried to keep my head down as much as possible. The military life I was hoping for began to fade much like all my other hopes and dreams.

Remember the young man I mentioned earlier whose mother Charlotte came to the graduation? His name was Derrick. He was in my company during bootcamp. He would help me with cleaning my weapons. We grew to like each other. Well, he was stationed aboard one of the Coast Guard Cutters in Mobile! The cutters were situated across town docked on Mobile Bay. My station was adjacent to the Mobile Regional Airport, so we were quite a distance from each other, still we found a way to get together.

In the beginning it was a nice change of pace. It took my mind off things. I now know that our budding relationship was a distraction from my relationship trauma I had endured and something to occupy my mind. Time went on, we dated, and eventually married all in the same year. It was beautiful.

Derrick was originally from East Orange, New Jersey. Well-mannered and soft spoken and extremely handsome. Lord when he put on those dress blues, my heart would stand still. He was pecan tan, muscular and smart! He would go out to sea at times for months. I remember picking him up from the docks once when he returned. A female friend, who had not yet met him, couldn't believe it when I pointed him out as he disembarked the ship.

She asked me, "where is he?"

I replied as I pointed in his direction, "there he is. The light skinned fellow."

She without hesitation said, "I know you lying! Why would a handsome guy like that want you?"

I couldn't speak. She insulted me and I couldn't speak. Who would want me?

Within a month of the marriage, I became pregnant with our first child, a boy. We named him Kevin. I was overjoyed and his daddy seemed to be as well. In addition to military life, I had a child to care for. Although he was my firstborn, I was a mother long before his arrival, having been the primary caretaker for my brothers.

As my belly grew, I could no longer fit my uniform and it was becoming a problem. I got in trouble every day for not wearing it properly. I could no longer fasten my skirt or trousers and so I would have to wear my blouse on the outside and I wasn't cut any slack. I had to continue working outside in the heat, picking up trash around the base, or working in the mess hall smelling bacon, which made me sick. I was growing tired of it all.

I used to think, *"God what did I do to have such a hard life?"* All I could think about was finding a way to get out. Derrick and I prepared for the arrival of our son. He was excited and so was I. We would fix up the nursery and Kevin had everything a baby needed!

During this time, which was 1975, Debbie and I had reconnected. She was living in Florida and had gotten my number from my stepmother. She came for a visit, and I met my niece, Stephanie for the first time. We didn't talk about mama, or what had happened. We embraced the moment and enjoyed each other's company. She let me keep Stephanie for a while and eventually returned to take her back to Florida.

Often on the weekend, Derrick and I would have guard duty. I knew once the baby came, and with no family in Mobile, it would be difficult to fulfil my military duties. I saw this dilemma as my way out. I requested a hardship discharge citing having no family in the area to care for the baby once he was born. The Commanding Officer was all too happy to approve that!

Within only a year of service, I was discharged. My discharged papers read, "Honorable Discharge due to the convenience of the government." That was in 1975 and those words still hurt. I felt like a failure. I had not obtained the wonderful military career I envisioned. I wore the shame of that like a garment for years. Many of my friends are just discovering that I am a five-point Honorably Discharged Veteran. I just wanted to put it all out of my mind.

Veronica was stationed in California and was living her best life. Julie got married and for a while, was doing great. This feeling of failing was another thing added on top of my head as if all the other crap weren't enough. It wasn't too long before this fairy-tale marriage began to crumble and crumble fast. He stopped liking me. I don't know why. He would say mean things, all the time. He had an affair. We separated briefly for six months and tried again. I found myself pregnant with another child, this time a girl. We named her Felicia. He said he didn't want to be a husband or a father, and when she was two months old, we separated for the final time.

Once again, I was on my own, this time with two small children. No mama to call. No sister to call. No one to call.

"The ultimate measure of a man is not where he stands in moments of comfort and convenience, but where he stands at times of challenge and controversy."

– Dr. Martin Luther King

CHAPTER EIGHTEEN

On My Own

Dad and my stepmother briefly separated, around 1977 and he called me and asked me if I would come home to keep the house going as he was still driving long distance. Against my better judgement, I agreed. I packed up my children and went back. I returned to Daytona feeling like a complete failure with two babies in tow, a broken marriage, and a very short-lived military career. Felicia was barely two months old, and Kevin was not two. It was rough I tell you no lie!

I've made no secret that there was no love lost between my father or stepmother and me. After a short period, my father and stepmother reconciled, and she returned home. Living in their house became an issue. Daddy and I had not had much of a father-daughter relationship and there was no bond between my stepmother and me. I needed to be on my own. I was made to feel that my children and I were in the way. My stepmother suggested that I could rent a room, across the street with a neighbor. So, I moved across the street, in a makeshift back room. I was working and I decided as soon as I can get bus fare, I'm out.

I ran into an issue while living with the neighbor and was told I had to move. With $30 in my pocket and two children, where was I going to go? I called my friend Yolonda to take me to a hotel. Believe or not, I got a room at the local Holiday Inn for $15 a night, used the other $15 to buy milk for my baby and food for Kevin and me. We settled in, and I cried all night.

When morning came, Yolonda picked us up. She dropped me off at the housing authority to see if we could obtain emergency housing. There was nothing available. I walked with the children to a bus stop and sat down. I had no idea what I was going to do. As night approached a young lady sat down beside me. I was in tears, and she spoke. "Hi. My name is Vanessa. What's wrong?'

Through my tears, I began to tell her my trouble. She then said, "come home with me."

I was shocked. She was a total stranger, and I couldn't impose. With a shaky voice I replied, "oh thank you, but I can't do that."

"Yes, you can, and you will. It's almost dark and I can't leave you and the children here. I have a good friend who lives next door, and she will know what to do. Please, come with me."

I did.

When we got to Vanessa's house, she went next door to get her neighbor. When the lady walked in, it was one of my childhood friends, Carrie Green. Carrie and I had grown up in the church in Daytona. She was as shocked to see me as I was to see her! She took me and the children in and I will never forget her kindness. We stayed for a short while huddled together in a one-bedroom apartment, but we made it work. Being there gave me time to think about what I wanted to do with myself and my children.

A short while later, Carrie began getting phone calls about us staying there from the management. I didn't want to get her into any trouble or cause her to lose her place. So, as I was making plans to go back to Mobile, I happened to run into my current husband's mother. She didn't know that I was back in town. I mentioned that I would soon be leaving, and she asked me why? I told her my dilemma and she invited me and the children to come live with her. I did. God bless her. After six months, I packed up the children and headed back to Mobile.

Upon my return, Derrick filed for divorce and that was that. The next few months, I did the best I could for us. I went back to school using my GI Bill. This bill was put into law to help honorably discharged veterans with education, purchasing homes as well as medical benefits. I cried a lot and hunkered down for the sake of my children. I was 21 years old, with two babies and all alone. It was scary. There were days that I thought I might not survive it all. But I would not abandon them! And with the grace of God, I did not. The love I had for them and the love they had for me, kept me sane.

Very quickly after the divorce I met a gentleman that would later become my second try at marriage. He had never been married and had no children. He wanted to be a part of our lives and asked me to marry him. So, I did. We married and again I found myself pregnant - with my last child. A boy we named JR. We managed to stay married for four years and then it was over.

I was twenty-three years old, single with three children! By this time, I had made a few friends, so it didn't feel so lonesome. I found a church home and was highly active there which occupied time. Things weren't so bad. So, for the next two years, it was me, my children and church.

Debbie called often during this time, and we were re-building our relationship. It was nice to have my big sister back in my life. But oddly, we did not talk about the things that had torn us apart. We were just being. I was twenty-seven, still living in Alabama while she was living in Fort Lauderdale, Florida. She called me one day to tell me that she had received word that our mother was ill and wanted to know if I wanted to see her!

The nerve! I said, "What for? I don't care whether she dies or not."

Debbie was flabbergasted. She said, "excuse me?"

I aggressively replied, "you heard what I said. Why should I? She never did anything for me. When I needed her the most, she was nowhere around; so, give me one good reason I should interrupt my life to see her?"

Debbie calmly said, "Regina, I don't believe you're acting like this. She's our mother!"

"Believe it!" I said defiantly, as I hung up the phone.

I was fuming after I hung up. How dare she call me out for not wanting to see that woman! She and I were trying to heal, and she had the nerve to try to make me feel bad for not wanting anything to do with a woman who didn't want anything to do with me!

Just as I was ranting, God reminded me of a prayer I said when I was younger. "God, please allow me to see my mother alive and not in a casket."

I picked up the phone to call Debbie. When she answered, I relented, "I will go with you."

Debbie was overjoyed. "Okay! I will check the bus schedule and call you back with the information."

"Okay," I said. "Talk to you soon. Goodbye."

CHAPTER NINETEEN

Hello Mommy, It's Gigi

Not long after I decided to listen to God and be obedient in going to see her, Debbie called me back with the information to travel to Hartford, Connecticut to visit our mother. By this time, it had been 21 years since I had seen her. What would I say? Would she even recognize me?

Finally, I could ask her some questions about why she left and never came back. Yep, it was going to be on and popping! I might yell at her or even curse at her, but I was going with the intent to get some straightening!

The bus Debbie put me on would leave Mobile with a stop and change in Savannah, Georgia. Debbie would be on that bus. I got someone to take care of the kids and I took pictures of them with me as she had never seen her grandchildren. I told God, "Let's do this."

I boarded the bus to Hartford and the memory of being on that double-decker Greyhound bus popped into my head. I had a seven-hour ride from Mobile to Savannah. I kept trying to picture what it would be like when I saw her for the first time after twenty-one years! Of course, I slept most of the way and that was a good thing. My brain was on overload, and I just needed to rest.

We finally pulled into the Savannah bus station. I was tired after that long ride. I got off the bus and the driver pointed me in the direction of the connecting bus. The layover wasn't long, and I was able to board after a few minutes. When I stepped on the bus everybody on there said, "Hi Regina!" I was stunned.

Debbie had talked to those passengers about me all the way from Fort Lauderdale! After my initial shock, I said "hello" and sat down in the seat beside her and off to Connecticut we went. I don't remember us talking much on the ride but I'm sure we did as we both had the gift of gab! This time we had a thirteen-hour ride from Savannah to Harford. We changed buses again in Washington D.C.

Prior to leaving for Hartford, my friend Janice remembered she had a friend there that might be able to put us up for the week that we were going to be there. She made a call and arranged it all. Once we arrived, we were met by the lady's son and taken to her home. I don't remember her name, but I know it started with a k. So, I will call her Miss K. It was late when we got there so we introduced ourselves, thanked her for putting us up and went to bed.

The next morning, we had breakfast and spoke briefly before we headed over to the facility where mom was. When we arrived, we walked into the building and took the elevator up to the floor she was housed on. I learned that the facility was a mental hospital and mom was there, on a secure floor. My first thought was, why is she in a mental hospital? Had she lost her mind? I didn't know what to think. My heart became heavy at the thought of her being locked away. I wasn't sure if Debbie knew this before we got there. If she did, she did not tell me. We were told she was there and on a secure floor because she accidently started a fire at the nursing home where she had been staying.

With this new information, my mind shifted from I'm going to get my answers, to, I hope these people are not mistreating her! I was gearing up to fight for her. Was there still some love for her in me? That moment illuminated the possibility. Still, I was apprehensive because I didn't know what to expect. The selfish part of me returned like a rush and I thought, if her mind is gone, I will never get answers.

When we got to the glass doors, we had to identify ourselves through an intercom.

"May I help you?" the lady asked.

"Yes, we are here to visit Elizabeth Redding," Debbie said.

The lady seemed shocked that Mama had visitors. We would later find out that absolutely no one was visiting her!

"Elizabeth?" she asked, as though she was dumbfounded.

"Yes," Debbie replied.

"And who are you?" She then inquired. Debbie was getting frustrated from all the questions.

"We are her daughters! I am Deborah and this is my sister Regina!" I thought Debbie was going to curse if that lady did not open that door. There was a loud buzz, and we heard the latch signifying we could push the door open. We went in. I was starting to feel nervous watching the exchange between Debbie and this woman. Debbie was a force to be reckoned with and I didn't want any trouble.

"We didn't know that Elizabeth had any children." The woman explained, apologetically.

"Well, she does," Debbie answered. "So, can we see her please?"

"One moment while I call her to come up front." I thought she was going to make a phone call or something but instead she called her name aloud, "Elizabeth!"

After several minutes, I heard this booming voice respond, "YEAH!" I was expecting this exceptionally large woman to appear matching the sound of her voice.

"You have a visitor." The woman advised.

"Be right there," Mama nonchalantly said.

We heard the shuffling of feet coming from the back towards us. Finally, the person with that booming voice stood in front of us.

"Yeah," she said.

There stood a petite woman no taller than me, and I am five feet. I could not believe my eyes! That big 'ole voice from that little lady?

"Yeah," she said again.

Debbie spoke because I didn't know what to say. "Mama, it's me, Debbie."

Mama looked at her for a moment and suddenly she recognized Debbie. You see unlike me, when Debbie got old enough, she sought mama out and was spending time with her throughout the years.

Mama began to cry, "Debbie? Oh, my baby." She hugged her. I watched, silently, waiting for my turn.

Then Debbie said, "Mama, look who is with me? You know her?"

Mama looked at me and then said, "no, I don't know her."

"Look at her real good mama. You know her." Debbie encouraged her.

By this time mama was getting irritated and so was I. She said defiantly, "I said I don't know her!"

I didn't know whether to slap her, curse her, or leave. Debbie could sense that I was about to do something, so she quickly said, "Mama, that's Regina, your baby."

Mama looked at me and said, "Regina! Oh, lawd, my baby!"

She grabbed me and started to cry. I wasn't moved by her tears. As a matter of fact, I was hurt that she didn't recognize me! I came for answers! Period! I hugged her back and we sat at the table in the sitting room.

The lady at the front desk asked me if I smoke. I answered, "Yes Why?"

She responded, "Please don't give her any matches."

I simply acknowledged her with okay. We sat at the table, and I was waiting for my chance to ask the one question I wanted an answer to all my life. Before I could do that, Mama asked, "You got a light?"

I looked at her and said, "yes."

"Let me see it."

To keep from giving it to her and not knowing how she would react, I said, "let me keep it so they won't take it from you."

That satisfied her for the moment, but two minutes later, she asked the same question. She asked for that light again and again and again!

Debbie sat quietly watching this exchange between Mom and me. I don't know what was going through her mind, but she knew how important this moment was for me. She didn't interrupt. I knew something was wrong and since her mind was gone that would mean she would not be able to answer my questions! I contemplated if I should attempt to ask her questions about her leaving. I was upset with God. I told Him softly within, *"God! Are you for real? I'm finally here and this is what's left?"*

Then she suddenly asked me, "your father still in Florida?"

"Yes," I replied.

"Uhm. He still preaching?"

"Yes," I replied.

"Uhm."

She asked me those two things, could she hold the lighter; and she would ask me about my father repeatedly.

Mama seemed to be stuck in time. And what was clear to Debbie and me, was the fact that she was stuck there with only the memory of our father. What could he have done to her for this to be her only thought? We were told by her doctor that she had suffered a diabetic coma. It affected her brain especially her cognitive abilities and her memory. I knew in that moment; it was a lost cause. I would never be able to get answers. I was crushed.

I really didn't know how to feel. I was just feeling a tremendous loss. The trip was all for nothing I felt.

We sat and let her ask those same questions and answered her the same way each time.

She then said, "I need to pee."

I said, "okay, I will go with you in case you need my help."

I took her in the bathroom and helped her pull down her pants and underwear and noticed the scar obviously from a c-section. So, I asked, "Mama, why do you have that scar?"

She replied, 'that's where you came from. You and Debbie and your brothers."

Wait, what? Hold the entire train! "I asked, my brothers? I don't have any brothers!"

She responded, "Yes you do. Two of them."

I had never heard that in my entire life. "Mama, what do you mean? Where are they?"

"They're dead" she said matter of fact.

"Dead? When? How did they die?" I was about to hit the floor.

"One lived a few hours after he was born, and the other boy was stillborn."

The shift from the conversation at the table to this one was remarkable! She was sharing information with me.

She continued, "there was a boy before Debbie and one after Debbie, then you."

I was speechless. I didn't know whether she was lucid enough to be telling me the truth or was everything just a fog in her mind. She said, "I'm done."

I helped her pull her underpants back up then her trousers. She washed her hands and back to the sitting room we went. She started again with the same questions about the lighter and my father. I was confused. We just had a whole conversation about my two dead brothers! Everything in me was screaming WHAT IS GOING ON?

I don't remember whether I told Debbie what she had said to me or not. There are still missing pieces to my story. We stayed a little while longer, then it was time to go. We promised her that we would be back the next day. She was fine with that promise, and we left.

When we returned to Miss K's house, where we were staying, we all sat and talked awhile. As we were talking, I was looking at the pictures around her house. I saw a picture of a woman who resembled my mother and I said, "this lady reminds me of my mother."

Amused, she said, "Really? That's my husband's cousin. What's your mother's name?"

Proudly I said, "Elizabeth Clay Hopkins-Redding."

She then said, "I think your mom is related to my husband!"

Her husband was deceased at the time, but she felt that there was a strong possibility that we were related. We spent the next several days going to visit mom and it was the same thing each day. The same two questions, and the same two answers. When it was time for us to head back to Alabama and Florida, I showed her the pictures of her grandchildren and decided to leave them with her.

I said, "you can keep those, and I promise when I come back, I will bring the children with me."

As we were saying our goodbyes, she began to cry and said, "please don't leave me here. Take me with you!"

Debbie calmly said, "Mama, we can't. You need medical care."

Mama began to wail and cry. I couldn't take it. Hearing her cry and plead like that, broke my heart. I wasn't the hurt little girl she had left so long ago. I wasn't angry or sad. My heart bled for my mama. And in that moment, I wanted to pack her up and take her with us. But instead, I asked them to buzz me out.

As I went through the doors, she ran after me and screamed, "please, please take me with you! What have I done to deserve this?"

The nurse ran out after her to try to restrain her, but Mama slapped her and was fighting with her while crying and wailing.

Debbie tried to console her and get her to calm down, all to no avail. I was beating on the elevator button so I could run. It seemed like forever before the door finally opened. As I stepped on the elevator, I could still hear her crying and pleading to go with us. I got off the elevator downstairs and waited for Debbie.

When Debbie finally came down, she was angry and crying. She said, "I'm going to get her out of there."

"How?" I asked, in disbelief.

"I don't know, but I will"

Debbie did speak with the doctor about us taking her back to Florida. Debbie was a Certified Nursing Assistant, so she had medical training.

The doctor advised her against it., "You won't be able to handle her. She's combative due to the coma she was in. She will require around the clock care."

Debbie assured him that she could do it. He refused to release mama. We were quiet on the cab ride back to Miss K's house. We would be leaving that next day. We talked briefly, met her children which we now believed were cousins and went to bed.

The next day, we left Hartford. I was headed back to Alabama while Debbie would travel on to Florida. The same way we came up, we would split up in Savannah. I went back home with more unanswered questions and that was the last time I would see my mother alive.

"*Unresolved issues will destroy your peace.*"

– Gigi Hodges

CHAPTER TWENTY

Life Goes On

I had seen her, and nothing was resolved so I once again, moved on with my life with a promise to get back to her when I could. In 1984, I married again but this time, no babies! The marriage was great. He accepted my children as his own and we had an amazing life together. He was strict but we had everything we needed. For a while.

A year after we married, Debbie received a phone call that mama wasn't doing so well. My husband at the time - Willie, Debbie, and I, took a road trip to Hartford. On the way we called her only sibling, my Aunt Ethel in Columbia, South Carolina. She asked us to stop through and pick her up so that she could go with us.

Auntie and Mama had been estranged for years. Auntie told me that my mama loved my aunts on my daddy's side more than her. I'm sure that wasn't altogether true but my mama's love for her sisters-in-law put a wedge between them. Mama and my paternal aunts partied together. That was the connection between them. She spent more time with them than she did with her sister and Auntie resented that even after Mama died.

One of my cousins on my daddy's side came to the wake service. Aunt Ethel gave her a message to take back to her family. "Tell your family, that they are not welcome here." I was floored.

I thought they had never reconciled but my cousin Francis, who is my Aunt Ethel's oldest daughter revealed in recent years that my mama went back to Columbia in the late 70s for a visit with Auntie. I was happy and relieved to hear that. We stopped in Columbia and made it to Auntie's house. It was October 8th, 1985.

When we walked in, my cousin Francis yelled, "Mama, Gigi is here." I turned to see who she was referring to and she said, "why are you looking like that?"

I responded, "who is Gigi?"

She laughed and said, "that's you! That's your nickname. My mama named you that when you were a baby!"

I had never heard that or been called by that name that I could recall. But I liked it.

Debbie called the hospital to tell them we were on the way. The hospital informed Debbie that there was no need for us to come. Mama had passed at 11:00 am that morning. Debbie asked the nurse if they would send any belongings to my aunt's address. She advised her that she had nothing there. Nothing? No clothes? What about the pictures of her grandchildren? The nurse was compassionate but adamant, "I'm sorry Miss, but she has nothing at the hospital."

It is unbelievable that a person could be born, live and die; and yet it appears as if they were never here. So instead of returning home, we stayed in Columbia and made funeral arrangements. We had her body brought back to her birthplace.

Mama was 50 years old when she departed this life. I suspect she was alone in that hospital, but I may never know. Debbie said it was Benny, her longtime friend who had initially called. I can only hope he was with her when she transitioned.

Her body was brought back to Columbia, and we prepared her homegoing services. It felt so strange sitting in the parlor for the wake with my mama's body lying there. The same age-old questions still swirling around in my head. I was willing her to wake up for a moment and have a talk with me. I know it sounds crazy, but I did. I cried, not about her dying, but because she died, and I didn't know her, and she never got to know me.

At the homegoing service, people I didn't know were giving us their blessings and prayers and afterwards we went to the cemetery for the committal. I watched as all the answers went into the ground that day.

Debbie and I became closer over the next several years. We spoke often and she would visit me in Mobile whenever she got the chance. She had become an over-the-road driver like daddy! Stephanie would come live with me, and my children, and I enjoyed having her with us. Debbie eventually took her back to Florida, but we were close by then.

I met Debbie's oldest daughter; Lula who had been raised by her father. Debbie had another daughter, Tammy who had been killed while following a group of older children into the street when she was only two years old. It was during this time, that she revealed to me the rape and how it destroyed her heart when daddy took her away.

I moved to Delray in 1992, at Debbie's insistence, following my divorce from Willie. In 2004, Debbie was diagnosed with cancer. We didn't visit quite as much during this time but in August of

2013, I felt the strong need to spend time with her. I had no idea it would be our last visit.

She was living in Georgia, and I spent two weeks with her there laughing, and watching westerns, especially "Tombstone" with actor Kurt Russell. Man, we both loved that movie!

We talked. We shared. We cried about how our lives had been. She mentioned how she felt when she was forced from our home. I cried for her. It took me a long time to know how much she loved me. I wish I could have been a better sister, a better friend.

She would succumb to cancer November 8, 2013. Then, my mama, my sister, and my father were all gone. I felt like I had fallen into a deep dark hole, and I was there all alone. The first people that I was connected to were all gone. I cried often after Debbie passed; and now, I still feel that disconnect, sometimes more profoundly than others. She was my living connection to our past. I miss her so much.

It would be 2016 before I would go back to Columbia to visit mom's gravesite. What I would have given to see her again.

Love is patient and kind; love does not envy or boast;
it is not arrogant or rude. It does not insist on its own
way; it is not irritable or resentful; it does not rejoice at
wrongdoing but rejoices with the truth. Love bears all
things, believes all things, hopes all things, endures all
things."

– 1 Corinthians 13:4-7

CHAPTER TWENTY-ONE

A New Dawn

In 2003, I was blessed to be reunited with a childhood sweetheart! My father passed away in February of that year and I went home to Daytona to prepare for his homegoing. My now mother in-law, Mary Hodges, was on the phone with my stepmother, Annie Mae.

As I walked into the house, I heard Annie Mae say, "she just walked in." I could only assume that Mamae (as Mrs. Hodges was affectionately called), had just asked about me.

Mom handed the phone to me, whispering who it was, and I smiled, "Hello Mamae! How are you?"

"I'm fine Regina." She responded. "I'm sorry to hear about your father. How have you been?"

I politely answered, "I am doing well thank you." Then I asked about her son Lamar who I had a fancy for when we were just young kids. "How is Lamar?"

"Oh, he is doing well." Her voice raised slightly, as though she was excited, I inquired about him.

"Where is he living now?" I inquired further.

She replied, "in Atlanta."

I said, "well please tell him I said hello." She said she would, and we ended the call.

My father and stepmother had five children together in addition to the three she had when they married, plus Debbie and me. Three of the children were born after I left home. Two boys and a girl. Lee, Josh, and Villa. I did not have the pleasure of being raised with them, but we were able to forge a relationship.

After the phone conversation ended with Mamae, I spent the evening with Villa and her family. She had a daughter, my niece Ta'Lani, and a baby son, Avery Jr. I was playing with Avery when I got a phone call from my brother Lawrence. He told me that a guy named Lamar had called the house looking for me and asked if I wanted the number.

"Of course," I said! He gave me the number.

I called and Lamar and I talked about old times. He apologized for not being able to attend the services for my father and he asked where I was living now and I told him, "Mobile, Alabama."

He said, "that's only a few hours from me. May I come over to see you when you get back?"

I suddenly felt like the 14-year-old girl who in 1970, had introduced herself to him from her bedroom window as he pulled into his aunt Ernestine's driveway. You see, his aunt lived next door!

"That would be lovely Lamar." I blushed.

We talked every day from that time until we finally met face to face.

We both knew instantly that we wanted to spend the rest of our days with each other, and it was clear that there was only one thing to do. We didn't need a long courtship. We were wise enough to know what we wanted. On July 26, 2003, we were married (me - for the last time)! God has blessed us to be together. God has used him to show me His perfect example of a man loving his wife like Christ loves the church. I have finally experienced unconditional love from this wonderful, sweet, kind, and gentle soul.

He has helped walk me the rest of the way, with patience, love and understanding. When he didn't have words, he held me when I cried, prayed for me when I felt overwhelmed all while showing me what it means to be loved. He is the ying to my yang! Make no mistake; we are not perfect, but we are perfect for each other. As of this writing, we have been happily married for more than a decade and a half! That is certainly a milestone for me. I had to learn that for healing to take place, there must first be a willingness to forgive. There have been wonderful revelations and transformations in my life for which I am profoundly grateful.

"For I know the plans I have for you, declares the LORD, plans to prosper you and not to harm you, plans to give you hope and a future."

– Jeremiah 29:11

CHAPTER TWENTY-TWO

Revelations

I was sitting having a cup of coffee and watching the wind blow through the trees just off my balcony, something happened. It was 2018. I was amazed at the fierceness of the wind and how one branch would bend and sway under the power of that wind. I was sure that it would break. I watched waiting for it to snap any moment. It never did.

God began to speak in my heart, and I heard these words, "that branch is you. The winds have blown mightily in your life and like that branch, you bent, and you swayed, and you bowed with every blow, but you DID NOT BREAK!"

I allowed my heart to hear God and as I continued to watch that branch, it sunk in deeper and deeper until the tears began to roll down my face. I thought about the things I had been through. All the hurt and the pain I suffered through. I thought about my failures, the disappointments, and the times I felt unloved, unwanted, disconnected from everybody and everything.

All my life I felt like I was dangling in the wind. Oh, I knew how to smile and be the life of the party but there was still the feeling of disconnect. And even in that, in this moment God was saying, "yes, all of that may be true, but you did not break!"

Until then, I had never publicly acknowledged my mother's wind. What her life may have been like. What things had she faced that were unbearable? Because God had my attention, He allowed me to see past my questions, past my pain, past my hurt and see my mama!

I had never considered *her* struggles until I allowed God to open my eyes to my own! I was too busy nursing my hurt to consider hers. She was a woman like me, dealing with life, like me. I imagine it was hard for her, like me.

Her alcoholism certainly contributed to her downward spiral and early demise. Benny, my mamas' friend, once told Debbie that mama never forgave herself for losing us and drank herself into an early grave.

After this revelation, I said aloud, "Mama, I'm sorry; and I forgive you."

I had never honored her on Mother's Day or her birthday after I dug into her abandoning us. But that year, 2018, to honor her memory, I decided to be called Gigi and so I changed my name to that on my social media platforms.

In 2021, my great-niece Briniesha piqued my interest and encouraged me to log onto Ancesstry.com to try to pull together our family tree. I did the thirty-day free trial and started popping in names. Information was coming up on my daddy's side and my mama's side and would you believe that I found a death certificate for one of my brothers! He was born May 11, 1953, right before midnight and only lived for 10 hours and 35 minutes! She was telling the truth! His name was Auzzie Lee Hopkins III. I couldn't believe my eyes. There was truth staring me right in the face!

I had rested the questions, but I guess God had not. God wanted me to have closure. The question still lingered however, why did she leave and never come back? Some of those questions got answered in a casual conversation with an older cousin on my father's side. I never knew that she knew my mother! My cousin Barbara called me one evening and we started talking about our family history. During that conversation, Barbara casually mentioned how nice Mama was and what an amazing dresser she was! Her hair had to be tight and everything exactly right!

She said, "your mom had lots of nice clothes and I used to go over to y'all house and ask her if I could borrow some and she would say 'go on in there and get what you want.'"

I was in awe. I began to cry, and I begged, "please tell me more. Was she funny? Could she sing?"

She said, "yes she was funny, and she did sing."

She told me things that I had never known before like the time she came to Florida for the summer not long after my father moved us there. She said, "I don't know why you don't remember."

So, I asked her, "how old were you then?"

She replied, "thirteen."

"I said that would mean that I was only three! That's why I don't remember!"

I shared with her what life had been like for Debbie and me and she began to cry. It was the most healing experience I have ever had.

By the time we ended the call, I was so full I thought I would burst. It was after midnight and my husband was asleep so I couldn't cry to him. I heard God say, sit down and let it all out. I cried for at least an hour.

I was so grateful for the information that my cousin shared with me. I finally felt some connection. She was funny, like me! She sang like me! She was a hairdresser, like me! She was together when she stepped out, like me!! Her hair was always tight, yep, like me! She was short, like me! It feels good to be maternally connected to someone who was like me!

When my daughter was 14, she used to wear her hair in this popular hairstyle known as a stack. It was tapered above the ears and stacked as it was cut to the crown of the head, leaving most of the length on top. I kid you not, the first time I saw the only picture of my mama I've ever seen, she was wearing that same hairstyle!

The only family members on my mother's side that I knew existed are my cousins, Aunt Ethel's children and a second cousin, Hazel. Since starting this journey, I have learned of a host of family! I have had the pleasure of meeting my second cousin, Lillie Boykin who is 80 years old! She is my mother's first cousin. Her mother and my grandmother were sisters! I have since met some of Lillie's family via Zoom! I cannot tell you how exciting this is.

I am so grateful to God for these truths that have found me. It is not everything about her, but it gives me a glimpse into who she was and, in my quest to know her, I discovered that our lives were parallel. We have similarities in fashion, we both were hairstylist and as I mentioned previously, we both sing. I also identify with the struggles of being a parent. That's a tough role. In seeking truth about her, I found truth about me and for now, that's enough!

Today, I accept her for who she is, what she was and whatever she desired to be. Mama, I forgive you. You did the best you could with the hand you were dealt.